LeadershipBytes

Elevate Your Leadership: 8 Effective Communication Skills

First Edition

www.versatileread.com

Document Control

Book Name	:	Elevate Your Leadership: 8 Effective Communication Skills
Document Edition	:	First Edition
Document Release Date	:	20th November 2023

Feedback:

If you have any comments regarding the quality of this book or otherwise alter it to better suit your needs, you can contact us through email at info@versatileread.com

Please make sure to include the book's title and ISBN in your message.

About the Contributors:

Abubakar Saeed

Abubakar Saeed is a trailblazer in the realm of technology and innovation. With a rich professional journey spanning over twenty-nine years, Abubakar has seamlessly blended his expertise in engineering with his passion for transformative leadership. Starting humbly at the grassroots level, he has significantly contributed to pioneering the Internet in Pakistan and beyond. Abubakar's multifaceted experience encompasses managing, consulting, designing, and implementing projects, showcasing his versatility as a leader.

His exceptional skills shine in leading businesses, where he champions innovation and transformation. Abubakar stands as a testament to the power of visionary leadership, heading operations, solutions design, and integration. His emphasis on adhering to project timelines and exceeding customer expectations has set him apart as a great leader. With an unwavering commitment to adopting technology for operational simplicity and enhanced efficiency, Abubakar Saeed continues to inspire and drive change in the industry.

Dr. Fahad Abdali

Dr. Fahad Abdali is an esteemed leader with an outstanding twenty-year track record in managing diverse businesses. With a stellar educational background, including a bachelor's degree from the prestigious NED University of Engineers & Technology and a Ph.D. from the University of Karachi, Dr. Abdali epitomizes academic excellence and continuous professional growth.

Dr. Abdali's leadership journey is marked by his unwavering commitment to innovation and his astute understanding of industry dynamics. His ability to navigate intricate challenges has driven growth and nurtured organizational triumph. Driven by a passion for excellence, he stands as a beacon of inspiration within the business realm. With his remarkable leadership skills, Dr. Fahad Abdali continues to steer businesses toward unprecedented success, making him a true embodiment of a great leader.

Afreen Iqbal

Afreen Iqbal is a talented and passionate content developer who breathes life into words. With an extensive background in content development, Afreen has honed her skills over the years, transforming ordinary words into immersive literary experiences.

Armed with a profound love for literature and a deep understanding of diverse genres, Afreen curates engaging content that resonates with readers across the globe. Her unique ability to blend creativity with insightfulness allows her to transport audiences into different worlds, each meticulously crafted through her words.

As a content developer, she continues to weave narratives that captivate, educate, and entertain. Her dedication to the craft and her passion make her an ideal guide on the path to leadership excellence, promising readers a delightful and enriching experience.

Table of Contents

About This Booklet

Welcome to Elevate Your Leadership: 8 Effective Communication Skills! This booklet is your express pass to mastering the art of effective leadership communication. Crafted for the modern professional in a fast-paced world, this guide condenses essential strategies and practical insights into a power-packed, concise format, allowing you to grasp the core concepts within just half an hour.

Why This Booklet?

In today's dynamic landscape, effective communication is non-negotiable for successful leadership. This booklet has been meticulously curated to address this need, offering practical and actionable advice that can be swiftly integrated into your leadership toolkit. It's designed for the go-getters who value time and want to enhance their communication prowess without investing lengthy hours in traditional courses or manuals.

What You'll Find Inside

This booklet is a comprehensive yet concise guide that covers crucial aspects of effective communication tailored specifically for leadership roles. From the importance of authentic communication and leveraging honesty to adapting messages to different audiences and planning for crisis, each section offers tangible strategies and practical tools. You'll discover how to communicate constructively, harness storytelling techniques, reinforce messages through body language, and much more.

How to Use This Booklet

The content is structured for quick absorption and immediate application. Each section is presented in bite-sized chunks, ensuring you can dive in, grasp key concepts, and implement strategies right away. Whether you're seeking to enhance your message, refine your presentation skills, or bolster your crisis management approach, this guide offers actionable insights in a concise, quick-to-read format.

Our Promise

This booklet isn't just about theoretical knowledge but real-world application. It aims to equip you with practical tools and techniques that you can seamlessly integrate into your leadership communication approach. By the end of this concise journey, you'll be empowered with actionable strategies to become a more effective communicator in your leadership role.

8 Effective Communication Skills

Introduction: Fast-Track to Leadership Stardom

Greetings, future trailblazers! Get ready to embark on a lightning-speed journey with our guide to 8 Effective Communication Skills, where we're about to transform your approach to leadership communication in; you guessed it, just 30 minutes!

In a world that moves at quantum speed, taking time for lengthy courses and exhaustive manuals is challenging. That's why we've crafted a power-packed, no-nonsense guide that delivers the essentials of effective communication straight to you in half an hour. We understand that you could be unlocking the secrets to becoming a communication maestro in the time it takes to grab a coffee.

Picture this: Elon Musk making split-second decisions, Steve Jobs captivating the world with a few choice words, or Michelle Obama inspiring millions with her eloquence. What do they have in common? They've mastered the art of communication. Now, it's your turn.

In this high-energy, action-packed course, we're not just going to teach you about leadership communication but immerse you in it. With real-life examples that read like page-turning stories and quick anecdotes that pack a punch, each section is designed to give you practical, hands-on tools that you can implement immediately.

From creating messages that resonate to conquering the email jungle and owning the stage with your voice, we've distilled the essentials into bite-sized, actionable chunks. This isn't about theory; it's about real-world application.

So, in the next 30 minutes, get ready to uncover your unique communication style, overcome challenges effortlessly, and measure success through tangible results. We're not just on a journey but on a mission to turn you into a communication ninja.

Fasten your seatbelt, set your timer, and let's dive into this 30-minute guide to mastering communication – because greatness doesn't need hours; it just needs the right 30 minutes!

The Importance of Communication

Our lives consist of interconnected feedback loops, meaning we are constantly communicating, whether we realize it or not. This communication can be intentional or unintentional; for most of us, it tends to be the latter. It's crucial to understand that our messages never exist in isolation; we always convey something, even in silence.

Reflecting on our communication habits presents an opportunity not to feel overwhelmed but to recognize the various elements at play. By identifying these components, we can gradually assume control, becoming more purposeful and conscious about how we express ourselves. Our communication methods are far from neutral; they either bring us closer to others or push us further away. They can even cause harm, necessitating subsequent repairs.

Considering the significant impact of every communication event, we are prompted to take action. We can seize control over even the smallest aspects of our communication. This empowerment lies in shaping our feedback loops intentionally, ensuring we receive better responses. These improved responses reinforce our positive behaviors, setting off a chain reaction of more positive feedback loops. In essence, our lives, as well as the lives of others, are shaped one positive feedback loop at a time, emphasizing the power of deliberate and thoughtful communication.

Three Crucial Communication Insights for Leaders

Understanding the key role communication plays in leadership is paramount for effective management. Here are three fundamental insights that underscore the essence of communication for leaders:

Authenticity Reigns Supreme:
The significance of authenticity cannot be overstated. It's about being genuine and transparent. Discover your unique voice, steering clear of corporate jargon or artificial personas. Your communication should reflect your background, values, and true self. People gravitate towards and trust authentic leadership. Prioritize authenticity over polished rhetoric; being real matters more than sounding perfect. Authenticity creates a connection, and people are unlikely to follow leaders they perceive as inauthentic.

Visibility Speaks Volumes:

Communication goes beyond written messages. It's about being accessible and visible. Emails and formal communications aren't sufficient; leaders need to be present and approachable. Consistently engaging and being visible showcases your leadership style. Building connections necessitates others seeing and feeling your leadership essence. Engage with all stakeholders regularly, particularly during challenging times like crises, to foster connections and trust.

Listening as a Potent Tool:

Effective communicators are adept listeners. Listening cultivates understanding and empathy. It's the gateway to trust, respect, and alignment. Actively listening, especially in coaching situations, is pivotal. Encourage open dialogue by allowing people to express their thoughts and concerns. Asking insightful questions opens avenues to genuine perspectives. Pay attention not only to spoken words but also to unspoken cues, fostering deeper understanding and trust.

The Power of Purposeful Communication

A strong communication strategy is the bedrock upon which successful marketing and communication initiatives stand. It's more than just a plan; it's a carefully crafted blueprint that defines focus, outlines clear objectives, and charts a roadmap for delivering messages that resonate and propel your audience into action.

As we embark on this quick guide, our mission is to explore the art and science of developing a robust communication strategy. We're not just covering theoretical frameworks; we're arming you with practical insights and a toolkit to create communication plans that are impactful, purposeful, and, most importantly, effective.

By the end of this guide, you'll be equipped with the knowledge and tools to communicate and, influence, inspire, and drive action. So, without further ado, let's learn the eight effective communication skills that leave an unforgettable mark!

Skill #1- Thinking Outside of the Box

Encouraging people to think beyond traditional boundaries often proves ineffective. A more successful approach to fostering creativity and problem-solving skills involves expanding the parameters within which individuals operate. Instead of urging them to think outside the box, presenting them with a larger conceptual framework is more fruitful. This approach compels the audience to contemplate ideas beyond their self-imposed limitations.

A compelling way to achieve this is by sharing a story about someone who demonstrated innovative thinking within a predefined context. Take the case of Tide, a leading laundry detergent brand in the US. In the late 1990s, the chemists and engineers at Procter & Gamble faced a challenge: a particularly stubborn type of dirt that resisted conventional cleaning methods and tended to transfer from one garment to another during washing. The typical obstacle in enhancing laundry detergent lies in balancing cleaning effectiveness and fabric safety.

However, the development team took a different approach. Instead of searching for chemicals to remove the dirt, they explored ways to prevent it from redepositing on the fabric. By shifting their focus, they discovered a solution that prevented the bonding reaction in the washing machine, ultimately creating the most effective Tide detergent ever produced.

This story illustrates a valuable lesson: sometimes, the most effective problem-solving method is to avoid the problem altogether. When your team faces a challenging issue, consider sharing this story and encouraging them to ask, "What if?" This approach encourages innovative thinking and opens the door to new possibilities.

Change Your Mindset for Growth

Is change possible? Absolutely, but the journey commences with a genuine desire for change. Embracing change involves recognizing your potential for transformation and, more importantly, understanding that accepting change enhances your ability to evolve.

This process doesn't entail abandoning your core identity; instead, it centers on growth and development, thinking outside the box. The concept of a growth mindset, pioneered by psychologist Carol Dweck, illustrates how individuals can hone their inherent characteristics, similar to athletes

refining their skills with coaches. Whether in virtual or office environments, proactive communication and learning initiatives demonstrate the essence of a growth mindset.

Consider your role as a leader. Are you someone who fosters connections and demonstrates personable leadership? Upon reflection, you'll realize that leadership isn't confined to the size of your team or the scale of your organization. Anyone interacting with others possesses influence, making them a leader in their own right. By embracing the growth mindset, you empower yourself to take control over aspects of your interactions that you may not have realized were within your grasp, encouraging innovative thinking. To transform yourself into a more personable and intentional leader, you must evolve, displaying purposeful interactions, genuine care, and mutual respect. This encapsulates the essence of growth leadership, laying the foundation for you to become the personable leader you aspire to be.

SMART Goals

1. Active Listening Workshops: Organize workshops emphasizing active listening, where leaders engage in discussions, debates, and role-playing exercises. Actively listening to diverse perspectives fosters open-mindedness and encourages out-of-the-box thinking.

2. Cross-Functional Collaboration: Initiate projects involving teams from different departments. Collaboration across varied expertise promotes creative thinking. Encourage brainstorming sessions to integrate diverse ideas and problem-solving approaches.

3. Diversity and Inclusion Training: Conduct training sessions on diversity and inclusion. Understanding different backgrounds enhances leaders' perspectives, encouraging innovative thinking. Facilitate discussions to celebrate cultural differences, fostering an inclusive environment where thinking creatively is valued.

Skill #2 – Leveraging the Power of Unfiltered Honesty

In the corporate world, two entities often bask in being right: your boss and your customers. Shaking things up and making an unforgettable impression on them sometimes involves saying the one word they least expect: "No." Let's have a look at the example of Gary Kaufer, a former executive vice president at an analytics company specializing in retail sales data.

In a meeting with a client, the CEO sought affirmation by asking, "I understand we're best-in-class among your clients using your data. Isn't that right, Gary?" Gary's response defied convention. He simply said, "No." The CEO, taken aback, inquired further, and Gary elaborated that the client wasn't fully utilizing the advanced analytical services included in their fee.

Gary's approach stems from years of experience, offering a unique third option for clients: confronting them about the value they're missing and then rectifying it. In another instance, he told a client, "You should fire us," a statement that prompted transformative discussions, enhancing both the client's business and his agency's success.

Incorporating such jaw-dropping candor into your communication can be remarkably effective. It's the rarity of this approach that adds shock value and amplifies its impact. Next time you encounter one of those self-affirming questions, consider trying it for yourself.

Communicating with Logic

Until relatively recently, our understanding of the brain and its role in regulating emotion and logic-driven communication was limited. In the 1980s, neuroscientist Antonio Damasio conducted groundbreaking research with a patient known as Elliot, shedding light on this aspect. Elliot had a portion of his frontal lobe removed during surgery to extract a tumor, resulting in the preservation of his high IQ but a loss of emotional capacity. This disconnection between logic and emotion rendered him incapable of effective communication and even simple decision-making. Effective communication necessitates the integration of emotional and logical thinking, as both are crucial aspects of our cognitive processes.

Emotional communication is rooted in sentiments such as pride, sympathy, ambition, and feelings, while logical communication hinges on clarity and rationality. This discussion primarily focuses on the latter—logical

communication. To communicate logically, one must construct arguments based on facts, present reasonable truth claims, and employ clear language. Although distinguishing between facts, truths, and opinions can be intricate and philosophical, practical purposes demand a simplified approach to enhance communication effectiveness.

- **Facts:** Objective information that exists independently of perception
- **Truths:** Claims based on subjective perceptions and reasoning
- **Opinions:** Matters of personal preference

Differentiating between facts, truths, and opinions enhances communication clarity, a fundamental goal when communicating logically.

SMART Goals

1. Critical Thinking Workshops: Organize workshops focused on critical thinking skills. These sessions can include exercises where participants analyze real-life scenarios, discerning between facts, truths, and opinions within the context of their organization. Engaging in group discussions and debates on these distinctions sharpens the ability to differentiate and communicate more clearly.

2. Fact-Checking Exercises: Introduce fact-checking activities within team meetings. Encourage team members to bring forward claims or statements related to their projects. As a group, fact-check these statements, discussing the sources of information and analyzing their validity. This exercise helps in developing a collective understanding of what constitutes a fact, truth, or opinion, fostering a culture of logical communication.

3. Interactive Case Studies: Create interactive case studies relevant to your industry or organization. These case studies should present complex situations where participants need to identify facts, truths, and opinions. Teams can collaborate to analyze the case, engaging in discussions to justify their categorization. This interactive approach strengthens the ability to apply the theory practically and reinforces the importance of clear communication grounded in logical thinking.

Skill #3 – Making Your Arguments More Constructive

In the year 1983, Joe Wilkie found himself in the shoes of an analyst at Nielsen BASES, a consumer research firm specializing in predicting the sales of upcoming products. The typical testing protocol involved presenting a new product concept to individuals in the first part, describing its functionality in just a few words. Subsequently, in the second part, participants would get hands-on experience with the product for a week or two, followed by a series of questions. Joe's initiation into this process led to unexpected results on one of his earliest projects. Participants rated the concept as average, but upon using the product, they expressed immense satisfaction—a notable disparity between concept and usage results.

Conventional wisdom might suggest launching a heavy sampling program in such a scenario, assuming that consumers wouldn't naturally try the product since the concept lacked appeal. However, Joe and his team had a more innovative idea. To implement it, they needed their client to acknowledge that one of its other brands had been falling short of promises made for years. This was no easy feat.

During the pivotal presentation, Joe's teammate took the stage, holding up a framed concept statement familiar to everyone. After reading it aloud, he dropped the bombshell—it wasn't the concept for the new brand. In fact, it was the concept tested three years ago for the client's previous brand in the same category. This revelation captivated the audience, leading to a discussion of the mediocre concept results and the stellar product outcomes. The explanation followed: the repeated promises in advertising over the years had eroded consumer trust. The concept, once loved, was now testing poorly because consumers no longer believed the brand could deliver on its assurances.

Instead of recommending the launch of a new brand, Joe's team proposed incorporating the innovative technology into the existing brand and finally delivering on the original promise. Remarkably, the client embraced this unconventional suggestion.

The key takeaway here is a lesson in making arguments more constructive. Instead of directly challenging the client's analysis and conclusions, Joe and his team reframed the issue by pointing out a flawed assumption. By doing so, they made it mentally and emotionally easier for the client to accept the

need for a change in plans. Contradicting assumptions is a powerful way to capture attention and secure agreement for unconventional recommendations. As Joe discovered, it paves the way for clients to be more open to transformative ideas without feeling defensive or foolish in the process.

Transform Conversations into Opportunities

Have you ever found yourself caught off guard in a conversation? Picture this: you believed the dialogue was heading in one direction, and suddenly, it took an unexpected turn, steering into uncomfortable territory and evolving into an unforeseen argument. Neuroscientists shed light on this phenomenon. Within the depths of our prefrontal cortex, neurons become less receptive to the opinions of others. Our brains struggle to process their arguments, irrespective of the quality of evidence supporting them. As we selectively overlook evidence that challenges our preexisting beliefs and actively search for supporting evidence, behavioral scientists dub this phenomenon "falling prey to confirmation bias."

Diverse cultural and individual perspectives shape our attitudes toward arguments. While some individuals relish the intellectual sport of debating, others may harbor a natural aversion, particularly if the discourse appears unconstructive and unproductive. However, this perception can transform when we recognize the value of a constructive argument. In such engagements, participants articulate their beliefs with solid reasoning, present considerations against opposing views, and evaluate the reasoning put forth by those who disagree. Arguments, when done correctly, become a means to navigate and understand complex issues collaboratively.

Approaching arguments from a critical thinking perspective reframes them from threats to opportunities for learning. The key lies in understanding that our comprehension of our opponents' viewpoints should originate from the opponents themselves, not filtered through those who share our beliefs. Establishing trust with your argument partner is essential. Begin by mutually agreeing to shift the goal from persuasion mode to understanding mode. Initiate the conversation by expressing your intent: "I'm eager to engage in this argument to understand your perspective. Let's first listen to each other and share our positions, reserving persuasion for later. Can we both agree on this approach?"

VERSAtile Reads

If your counterpart agrees, proceed by inviting them to go first. If the initial goal of understanding is not accepted, the conditions for a constructive argument are not in place. When both parties agree, the benefits are profound: a deeper understanding of your own beliefs, enhanced insight into the perspectives of those with opposing views, a diversity of ideas, stimulation of innovation, and the revelation that you may be mistaken.

Surprisingly, the acknowledgment of being wrong is presented as a valuable outcome. Constructive arguments serve as a practice ground for recognizing and learning from our errors. This openness to the possibility of being wrong, albeit initially uncomfortable, contributes to continuous improvement and the refinement of our knowledge. It's an investment in your cognitive bank, a process that might initially sting but ultimately fosters growth and wisdom.

SMART Goals

1. Argumentative Dialogue Circles: Establish regular dialogue circles where team members engage in structured argumentative discussions. Create a safe space where individuals can openly present their viewpoints and actively listen to opposing perspectives. Rotate roles within these circles, allowing everyone a chance to initiate discussions and facilitate constructive dialogue.

2. Cross-Team Debate Sessions: Arrange debate-style sessions between different departments or cross-functional teams within your organization. Assign topics relevant to the organization's challenges or industry trends. Encourage teams to research, prepare, and present their arguments in a structured format. Emphasize the importance of respectful discourse and active listening during these sessions. Afterward, hold reflective discussions to highlight the strengths of various arguments and insights gained from opposing viewpoints.

3. Argument Review: Introduce argument review sessions as part of team meetings. Encourage individuals to bring forward recent arguments they've engaged in or witnessed. Facilitate a collective discussion where the team analyzes these arguments objectively, focusing on how well each party listened, presented their viewpoints, and considered opposing opinions. This exercise encourages reflection and reinforces the principles of constructive argumentation.

Skill #4 - Adapting the Message to Your Audience

Sara Mathew stepped into her role as chief financial officer at Dun & Bradstreet in August 2001, unaware of the impending challenge. Less than a year later, she uncovered a significant issue plaguing the company's financial records: a persistent overstatement of revenues due to erroneous application of accounting rules. The task at hand was daunting—a comprehensive restatement of financial records spanning several prior years, all required within a mere six-week window before the next quarterly earnings release.

The finance and accounting teams embarked on an arduous journey, enduring long days that often extended well into nights and weekends to rectify the errors promptly. Their unwavering dedication and precision instilled confidence among Wall Street analysts, averting the expected drastic drop in the company's stock price.

However, the aftermath of this tumultuous period brought an unexpected revelation. The annual employee satisfaction survey painted a disheartening picture: Sara's department ranked the lowest across the organization. This feedback served as a stark indicator of the toll that the intense focus and extended hours had taken on employee morale. It was a concerning development that even drew the CEO's dissatisfaction.

In a candid conversation, the CEO confronted Sara about her leadership. Initially disappointed by the survey results, Sara attempted to justify her actions, believing the ends had justified the means. However, the CEO's resonant statement challenged her perspective: "Great leaders, Sara, do both." This profound insight triggered a profound reflection on her leadership approach and its impact on others amid her enthusiasm for delivering results.

Sara acknowledged her strengths in strategic thinking and problem-solving but recognized her shortcomings: a lack of empathy, an overly direct demeanor, excessive demands, and an intensely competitive nature. She had always assumed these traits were intrinsic to her effectiveness, but this experience changed her view. Encouraged by her boss, Sara initiated open discussions with her team to solicit direct feedback on her leadership style. It was a humbling and uncomfortable process, but one she embraced with `open arms.

In the process of feedback collection, she realized a critical aspect she had overlooked—adapting her message to her audience. Her overly direct communication style didn't resonate well with her team. Sara's approach lacked empathy, which made her appear unapproachable, particularly in times of high stress.

Armed with this new insight, Sara not only gathered valuable feedback but also implemented actionable changes. Over the following two years, her department's employee satisfaction scores soared, making it one of the highest-ranked teams in the company.

Sara's journey underscores the paramount importance of becoming a learning leader. Irrespective of past success or organizational stature, continuous learning remains a cornerstone for effective leadership. This transformation propelled Sara from CFO to CEO and board chair, signifying the significance of self-awareness and adaptability in leadership. Adapting the message to resonate with the audience emerged as a pivotal learning point in her journey—a testament to the enduring value of continuous growth and adaptation for successful leadership.

Navigate Multi-Channel Communication for Impactful Reach

Refine your communication strategy to echo across diverse channels. Consider this: where you relay your messages matters just as much as the content itself. Constructing an audience-centric strategy demands an understanding of what your audience desires and where they engage with information. Pinpointing these preferred channels is pivotal as you dissect each audience segment.

Divide your approach into three fundamental communication channels: owned, earned, and social. Your "owned" channels include platforms under your organization's control—such as websites, emails, newsletters, and advertising. "Earned" channels involve attention garnered from external sources, like media coverage or news websites mentioning your organization. Then there are "social" channels, encompassing both your organization's platforms (like YouTube or Instagram) and those of others.

Owned channels serve as hubs for shared information, anchoring your audience to your platforms. Meanwhile, earned channels are apt for newsworthy content or reaching fresh audiences, demanding adeptness in media engagement. Social channels, where information spreads virally,

require nuanced strategies per platform; tailor your content to match each platform's strengths.

While search engines overlap these categories, focusing on owned, earned, and social channels molds your communication strategy's implementation. Ensure your content resides primarily on owned platforms, utilizing earned channels for impactful news or community engagement initiatives. Social channels thrive on brand activity, spreading your message—choosing platforms that align with your content's nature boosts visibility.

Navigating this terrain requires a steady pace. Initiate your social presence gradually, starting with one or two platforms. Cultivate a robust community before expanding to multiple platforms, ensuring consistent and thoughtful content delivery. The goal? A cross-channel strategy ensures your messages resonate across owned, earned, and social channels, maximizing your message's extensive reach.

SMART Goals

1. Channel Assessment Workshop: Organize a workshop involving key team members responsible for communication. Task them with mapping out the existing communication channels used by the organization, categorizing them into owned, earned, and social. Discuss the effectiveness and strengths of each channel for disseminating information. Brainstorm strategies to optimize these channels based on the nature of content and target audience.

2. Platform-Specific Content Creation Challenge: Encourage your team to engage in a content creation challenge. Divide them into groups and assign each group a specific social media platform. Challenge them to create content tailored explicitly for that platform, considering its unique characteristics and user base. This activity fosters a deep understanding of platform dynamics and how content can be optimized for different channels.

3. Cross-Channel Strategy Simulation: Facilitate a simulation exercise where teams develop a hypothetical communication strategy for a new initiative or campaign. Encourage them to plan how the information would be disseminated across owned, earned, and social channels. Emphasize the importance of seamless integration and consistency in messaging across these channels. Encourage feedback and evaluation to refine the strategy.

Skill #5 - Differentiating between the Tangible and Abstract

Back in 2006, a major retailer approached its top supplier to dive into a key customer category: the achiever moms—those formidable Type A personalities managing homes like enterprises. Instead of following the conventional route with orderly PowerPoint slides, the supplier opted for an innovative approach. They introduced Julie, one of their own, who impeccably embodied the profile of an achiever mom. Sitting in the center of the room, she personified the abstract concept they were discussing.

The supplier's team leader invited the audience to engage with Julie by asking questions. Initially hesitant, the queries soon poured in: shopping habits, preferences, and buying choices. Julie's responses, derived from both research findings and her personal experiences, captivated the audience. By the session's end, the retailer's management gained an in-depth understanding of the achiever mom segment.

This unique presentation strategy paid off remarkably. The retailer's management, through direct interaction, not only posed their queries but also uncovered new insights beyond the supplier's agenda. The encounter led to a profound organizational change, restructuring the management around key customer segments.

The dichotomy between the abstract concept of the achiever mom and the tangible embodiment in Julie became evident. This distinction prompted the retailer to revamp its management structure, creating dedicated roles for each target segment. When the position of Senior VP for the achiever mom segment arose, the retailer explicitly desired Julie, acknowledging her as the living epitome of the segment.

Julie, renowned for her marketing brilliance, had previously declined offers from the retailer. However, her embodiment of the achiever mom's identity made her indispensable. The retailer, determined to have her, eventually succeeded in temporarily borrowing her from the supplier to spearhead the segment.

Employing concrete representations—like Julie in this instance—helps bridge understanding gaps, making concepts more tangible and engaging for the audience. By creatively transforming the abstract into the concrete,

your ideas resonate more profoundly, ensuring a more profound impact on your audience.

Listen and Lead with Conviction

Listening and actively encouraging input is foundational to effective leadership. Engaging individuals across all levels of the organization, from key stakeholders with diverse opinions to new employees who might hesitate to speak up, fosters an inclusive environment. Demonstrating that every individual's perspective is valued creates a sense of psychological safety, making it easier for team members to voice their concerns. This approach reinforces the importance of both tangible and abstract elements within the organization.

Acknowledging the value of every team member's contribution showcases genuine care for both individuals and the organization's collective success. Empathy plays a pivotal role in creating an atmosphere where individuals feel heard and understood.

Embracing silence is another crucial aspect of effective communication. Encouraging others to share their thoughts and ideas before presenting your own demonstrates respect and promotes an environment where everyone's input is valued. Practicing active listening, with a ratio of 80% listening and 20% speaking, exhibits a genuine interest in understanding your colleagues. This approach builds trust and strengthens the emotional connection necessary for effective leadership.

Leaders can create a well-rounded environment that fosters open communication, innovation, and mutual respect by differentiating between tangible aspects, such as the opinions and ideas shared, and the more abstract, emotional elements like trust and psychological safety.

SMART Goals

1. Diverse Roundtable Discussions: Regularly organize roundtable sessions that bring together diverse teams to collectively tackle specific challenges or generate innovative ideas for new projects. Designate a moderator to ensure every participant has an equal opportunity to express their thoughts, fostering an inclusive environment where all voices are valued. Encourage active engagement from all team members, regardless of their seniority, to freely contribute their unique perspectives and ideas.

2. Empathy in Action: Initiate an exercise focused on building empathy among team members by pairing them up to share personal stories or experiences that have shaped their perspectives. After this sharing, encourage reflection on how this exercise influenced their understanding of their colleagues' viewpoints. Discuss as a team how empathy can significantly enhance collaboration and communication within the group.

3. Silent Idea Generation: Organize a silent brainstorming session where team members jot down their ideas on sticky notes or a shared digital platform, without immediate discussion. Subsequently, prompt a discussion where each participant elaborates on their ideas without interruptions. Encourage active listening by emphasizing the importance of understanding each idea thoroughly before presenting their own thoughts.

Skill #6 – Illustrating through Stories & Metaphors

Alltel Corporation, established in 1943, grew to be a significant wireless telecommunications provider by 2007. During that time, the CEO, Scott Ford, faced a pivotal moment when the company was being sold to private equity firms. Rather than presenting the anticipated charts and graphs, Scott arrived with just two slides, one featuring a commonplace image of a person entering a yellow cab on a bustling New York City street, a sight familiar to the Goldman Sachs team.

Private equity firms aim to elevate the value of acquired companies swiftly and sell them off. Scott's presentation employed the metaphor of hailing a yellow cab to explain the confluence of events needed to sell the company for a higher value. He detailed the necessity of a big carrier buyer, low interest rates, and a conducive political climate in Washington DC to allow a substantial acquisition.

A year later, an executive contacted Scott regarding a $28.1 billion offer from Verizon to buy the company. In a phone conversation, Scott remained silent, prompting the executive to realize that this was indeed the opportune moment, the "yellow cab" moment as previously described. This executive recognized that all three criteria Scott highlighted were aligning, leading to the decision to accept the offer without further deliberation.

Scott's adept use of the yellow cab metaphor influenced the executive to seize the present opportunity rather than wait for a potentially better one. Metaphors like these leverage existing stories in the audience's mind, allowing ideas to be remembered long after they're initially presented.

Use Stories to Breathe Life into Vision and Leadership

When you immerse a vision, goal, or objective within a compelling story, it takes on a life of its own. Stories are the vessels that transport these ideas, not merely as concepts but as vibrant, relatable experiences. They're the heartbeat of communication, fostering trust, captivating minds, and eliciting emotional connections. Unlike referencing a mission statement, strategy document, or project plan, stories have an innate ability to linger, deeply etched in people's memories, readily recalled and retold.

Crafting a good story isn't just about narrative; it's about channeling authenticity, passion, and conviction into a tale that resonates. These stories

serve as a beacon, continually reminding individuals of the overarching vision. They encapsulate complex ideas, making them relatable and understandable to diverse audiences. This approach doesn't just inform; it inspires action.

In the realm of leadership, storytelling is more than a communication tool; it's the cornerstone of a leader's brand. Your capacity to articulate a compelling and authentic narrative reinforces your credibility and authority. A well-crafted story shapes perceptions, aligns values, and garners support. It humanizes the vision, fostering a shared sense of purpose and commitment among your team or audience. It's the difference between merely stating objectives and instilling a belief in a collective journey toward a common goal.

SMART Goals

1. Storytelling Workshop: Organize a workshop focused on storytelling techniques for your team or organization. Invite a professional storyteller or a communication expert to lead the session. Engage participants in interactive exercises that involve crafting stories around organizational goals or visions. Encourage them to infuse personal experiences and emotions into these narratives. Provide constructive feedback to enhance the impact of their storytelling.

2. Story Circles: Initiate regular story circles where team members gather to share personal or professional experiences related to the organizational vision or objectives. Create a safe space for individuals to share their stories, emphasizing the elements that evoke emotions or align with the overarching narrative. Rotate the facilitator role to encourage active participation from different team members. Encourage active listening and reflection after each story, discussing how these narratives connect with the shared vision and values.

3. Story Mapping Exercise: Conduct a collaborative activity where teams visually map out stories that represent various aspects of the organizational vision or goals. Provide prompts related to key milestones, challenges, successes, or values. Encourage teams to illustrate these stories through drawings, diagrams, or timelines on a shared board or digital platform. Afterward, have each team present their story maps and discuss how these narratives align with the broader organizational narrative.

VERSAtile Reads

Skill #7 - Reinforcing Intent with Body Language

Jane was the CEO of a growing technology company, and her leadership style was defined by her unwavering commitment and passion for her team's success. Despite her eloquence in verbal communication, Jane understood the power of non-verbal cues in conveying messages effectively.

During a pivotal quarterly meeting with stakeholders, where the company's strategic direction for the upcoming year was to be presented, Jane was acutely aware that her body language would significantly influence how her vision and intent were perceived.

As she stepped onto the stage, her posture was erect yet inviting, radiating confidence and approachability. She maintained steady eye contact, demonstrating her sincerity and engagement with the audience. Her gestures were purposeful and aligned with her words, emphasizing key points without overpowering the message.

During critical moments in her speech, where she emphasized the company's core values and the importance of innovation, her open palms and expansive arm movements signaled transparency and enthusiasm. When discussing the challenges ahead, her slightly furrowed brow and empathetic facial expressions conveyed understanding, while her reassuring nods projected confidence in overcoming obstacles.

Jane's mastery lay not just in her words but in the seamless synchronization of her body language with her intent. Her movements were deliberate, amplifying her message's emotional resonance. Her open and welcoming posture invited collaboration and trust, while her subtle cues of determination and conviction inspired confidence in the company's direction.

After the meeting, as Jane interacted with attendees, her warm and firm handshake, coupled with genuine smiles and attentive listening, further solidified the trust and respect she garnered from her team and stakeholders.

Jane's conscious effort to align her body language with her words and intent left a lasting impression. Her ability to communicate with her voice and through her presence and gestures exemplified how reinforcing intent with body language can amplify the impact of a leader's message and foster a deeper connection with their audience.

The Importance of Body Language

Our ability to interpret body language is innate, yet often, we overlook how we convey it ourselves. In a revealing incident, a client, disconcerted by feedback suggesting disengagement in meetings, insisted that she was genuinely interested. Upon observation during a series of all-hands meetings, she remained unaware of her closed-off posture—arms folded, chin down, appearing disinterested or even hostile. This incident highlights the significance of being purposeful in our non-verbal communication to understand the subtle ways we constantly convey messages.

Let's dive into some specific techniques to take ownership of our body language, deliberately demonstrating care and value toward our audience. Posture, the silent communicator, speaks volumes. Whether sitting or standing, our posture conveys interest and energy. Leaning slightly forward signifies engagement, while leaning too far back might appear disinterested or too relaxed. Mindful standing or sitting posture communicates focus to your audience and prompts you to maintain focus within yourself.

Gestures also play a crucial role in effective communication. Your gestures should be visible within the camera range during virtual interactions, indicating care and connection. Avoid forceful or authoritarian gestures; opt for open and compassionate gestures that align with purposeful and compassionate leadership styles.

Facial expressions significantly contribute to audience perception. Your expression sets the tone for how your message is received. A warm smile and engaged eyebrows convey care and enthusiasm, enhancing the receptivity of your audience.

It's important to note that body language is interpreted holistically. An isolated gesture or posture might not convey the intended message. For instance, crossed arms might not signify defensiveness if paired with a broad smile. Consistency, context, and unity in our body language create a more comprehensive picture. Layering these aspects—posture, gestures, expressions—gradually over time allows for a more authentic and impactful communication style.

By taking ownership and gradually incorporating these techniques, we can effectively communicate care, enthusiasm, and value through our body language, creating a consistent and genuine cluster of non-verbal cues.

SMART Goals

1. Mirror Exercise: Pair up with a colleague and take turns leading and mirroring each other's body language. Set a short timer and consciously adjust your posture, gestures, and facial expressions while the other person mimics your movements. Swap roles and repeat. Afterward, discuss what felt effective and what could be improved, fostering awareness and refinement of non-verbal cues.

2. Record and Reflect: Record yourself during a presentation or conversation. Review the recording to assess your body language—posture, gestures, and facial expressions. Identify habits that enhance or detract from your message. Set improvement goals based on observations and work on refining non-verbal cues in subsequent recordings.

3. Non-verbal Feedback Session: Host a team meeting focused on non-verbal communication. Ask participants to note down observations about a leader's body language during a brief speech or discussion. Collect anonymous feedback on posture, gestures, and facial expressions. Discuss the observations as a group, highlighting effective and less effective cues, allowing leaders to reflect and improve on their non-verbal communication skills.

VERSAtile Reads

Skill #8 – Planning for Crisis

Procter & Gamble's journey with Pringles began as a roaring success in 1971, swiftly becoming a household name by 1975, selling 10 million cases annually and claiming a 15% market share. However, the subsequent years brought a staggering downturn—a 20% sales drop, then another 10% the following year. Such rapid decline often signals panic for brand managers. The outlook seemed dire, and discussions about selling the brand surfaced by 1978.

The situation deteriorated further by 1979, with Pringles facing a steep 30% sales plummet, dwindling to a mere four million cases yearly—a 60% nosedive in four years. It was a turning point for P&G's executives, who set a five-year ultimatum: either resurrect or divest the brand. Over the next 18 months, strategic changes were implemented—rigorous consumer research, product enhancements, revamped advertising, and competitive pricing strategies.

The impact was tangible. Though sales continued to dip, the rate of decline significantly slowed down. Sales reduced to 3.4 million cases in 1980, bottoming out at three million in 1981. However, a progressive shift ensued, with sales gradually escalating to five million cases in 1984 and reaching seven million by 1986. By 1989, Pringles had restored its sales to the peak of 10 million cases in 1975 and surged further in the late '90s, exceeding 50 million cases.

In a pivotal speech in December 1984, Mike Milligan, P&G's sales head, articulated five lessons from this transformative journey. While the first three lessons underscored consumer understanding, aligning products, and forming robust teams, the fourth lesson stressed setting realistic, long-term goals amidst crises. However, the pivotal takeaway was encapsulated in two words: "Don't stop." P&G's persistence against immense sales declines, resisting the temptation to abandon Pringles, underscored the importance of crisis planning and persevering to rectify the business.

This contrasted starkly with modern CEOs fixated on quarterly profits, often opting for immediate exits at the first sign of trouble. Pringles emerged as a testament to resilience and courage within P&G's brand portfolio. Thomas Edison's wisdom echoed profoundly: "Many of life's failures are people who didn't realize how close they were to success when they gave up." The crucial

lesson? Perseverance amidst crisis and staying committed to eventual success.

Build Resilience through Strategic Planning

Crises range from minor disturbances to major upheavals. Some crises fizzle swiftly, while others morph into persistent obstacles eroding an organization's relationships with stakeholders. The linchpin to effective crisis management lies in comprehensive crisis communications planning. While predicting the unpredictable is challenging, establishing robust framework arms you with the ability to navigate tumultuous situations with clarity amid chaos.

Integrating crisis preparedness into your communication strategy starts with scenario planning. Gather your team or organization's essential members for a brainstorming session. Dive into potential issues based on your business, industry landscape, customer segments, and partnerships. The aim here is an unrestricted exchange of conceivable scenarios. Following this, prioritize scenarios based on their potential impact on your business, customers, and employees.

Once you've identified these critical scenarios, begin crafting response plans: What to communicate, who should be your primary spokespersons, how to address and rectify the issue, timing and frequency of communications, and the most effective channels to reach your audience. This proactive approach enables swift action and a coordinated response when a crisis strikes. Even if the crisis you face isn't one you've precisely scenario-planned for, this exercise will have honed your critical thinking, facilitating a quicker and more effective response.

Transparency stands as a pivotal principle in crisis communication. Avoiding cover-ups is paramount; instead, embrace accountability and transparency. Acknowledge mistakes upfront, as owning up to them is the first step in regaining trust. Maintaining openness with your audience fosters trust and loyalty, even during turbulent times.

Planning for crises is a non-negotiable component of a robust communication strategy. It positions you to act decisively and ethically, safeguarding your organization's interests and relationships with stakeholders. Integrating crisis preparedness into your communications strategy is not just beneficial—it's imperative.

SMART Goals

1. Scenario Brainstorming Session: Gather your team representing diverse perspectives within your organization. Engage in an open discussion, exploring potential crisis scenarios relevant to your industry, business landscape, and stakeholders. Prioritize these scenarios based on their potential impact. Then, strategize and outline response plans, including communication strategies, key spokespersons, rectification actions, and effective communication channels.

2. Response Simulation Drill: Create a simulated crisis scenario based on the prioritized scenarios. Assign specific roles to team members and conduct a tabletop or virtual exercise where they respond to the simulated crisis. This practical drill enables team members to practice their crisis communication strategies, assess their readiness, and identify areas for improvement.

3. Post-Incident Review and Adaptation: Following the crisis response simulation, convene the team for a thorough review. Evaluate the strengths and weaknesses of the response, encouraging open dialogue to identify areas for enhancement. Use these insights to update and refine the crisis communication plan, ensuring continuous improvement and readiness for future crises.

Wrapping Up

Congratulations! You've just completed our lightning-paced guide to 8 Effective Communication Skills, where we've condensed the essentials of leadership communication into a power-packed half-hour. Let's recap the key points we've explored on this exhilarating journey:

- **Thinking Outside of the Box:** Embrace creativity and innovative thinking in your communication style.
- **Leveraging the Power of Unfiltered Honesty:** Authenticity is key. Avoid corporate jargon and be true to yourself to build trust.
- **Making Your Arguments More Constructive:** Craft your messages in a way that they're constructive and facilitate understanding rather than causing confusion.
- **Adapting the Message to Your Audience:** Tailor your communication to resonate with diverse audiences, understanding their needs and preferences.
- **Differentiating between the Tangible and Abstract:** Balance concrete information with abstract concepts to create a comprehensive message.
- **Illustrating through Stories & Metaphors:** Use storytelling and metaphors to convey complex ideas in a relatable and engaging manner.
- **Reinforcing Intent with Body Language:** Align your verbal communication with non-verbal cues to strengthen your message.
- **Planning for Crisis:** Be proactive in crisis management by scenario planning and preparing responses, ensuring transparency and accountability.

Remember, communication isn't just about words; it's a strategic tool crucial for effective leadership. With these key insights at your fingertips, you're equipped with the right tools to communicate effectively, authentically, and strategically. Your journey to becoming a communication maestro has just begun!